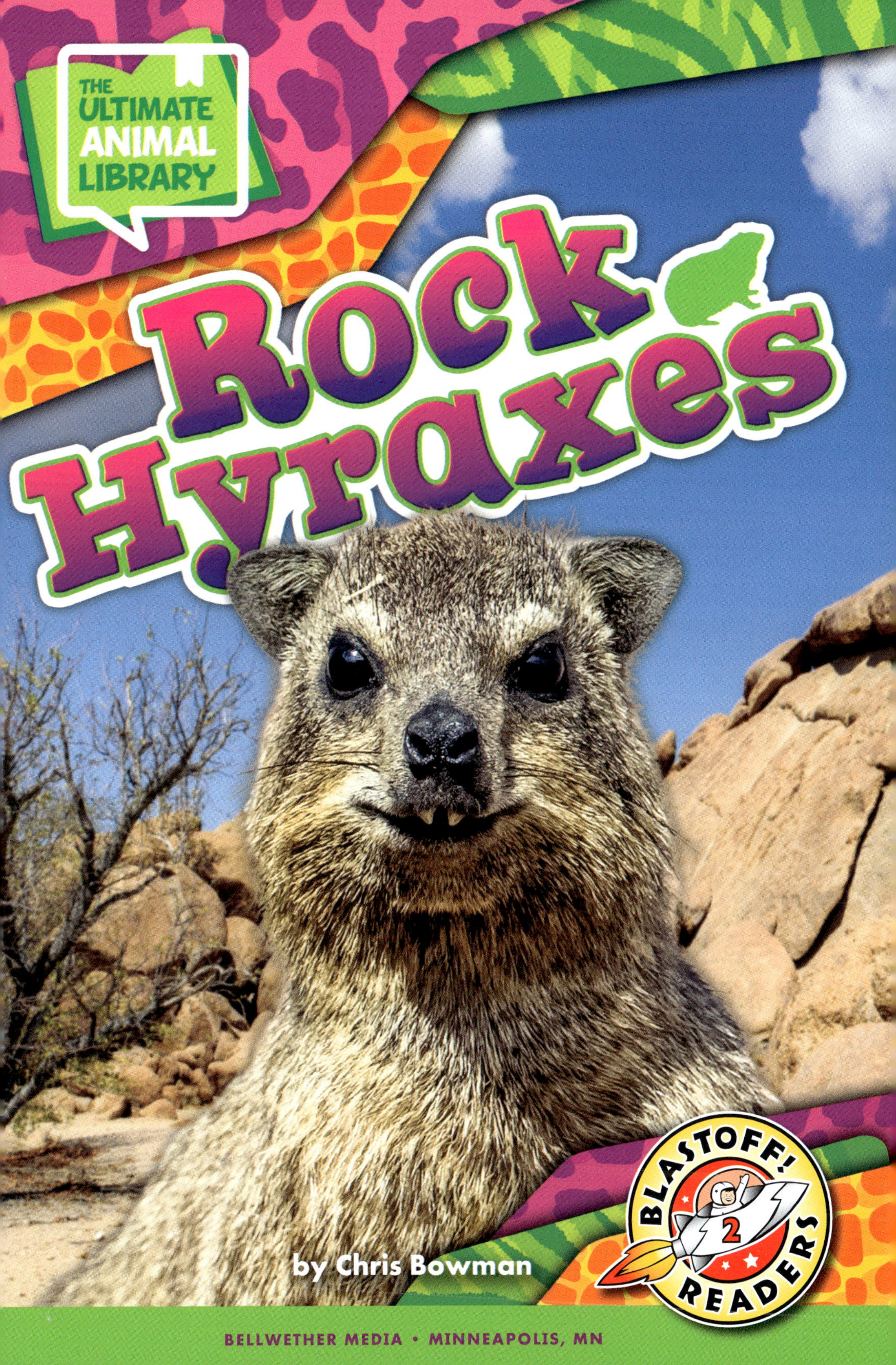
THE ULTIMATE ANIMAL LIBRARY
Rock Hyraxes
by Chris Bowman
BLASTOFF! 2 READERS
BELLWETHER MEDIA • MINNEAPOLIS, MN

Blastoff! Readers are carefully developed by literacy experts to build reading stamina and move students toward fluency by combining standards-based content with developmentally appropriate text.

Level 1 provides the most support through repetition of high-frequency words, light text, predictable sentence patterns, and strong visual support.

Level 2 offers early readers a bit more challenge through varied sentences, increased text load, and text-supportive special features.

Level 3 advances early-fluent readers toward fluency through increased text load, less reliance on photos, advancing concepts, longer sentences, and more complex special features.

★ **Blastoff! Universe**

Reading Level

Grade K

Grades 1–3

Grade 4

This edition first published in 2025 by Bellwether Media, Inc.

Library of Congress Cataloging-in-Publication Data

Names: Bowman, Chris, 1990- author.
Title: Rock hyraxes / by Chris Bowman.
Description: Minneapolis, MN : Bellwether Media, Inc., 2025. | Series: Blastoff! readers. The ultimate animal library | Includes bibliographical references and index. | Audience: Ages 5-8 | Audience: Grades 2-3 | Summary: "Relevant images match informative text in this introduction to rock hyraxes. Intended for students in kindergarten through third grade"-- Provided by publisher.
Identifiers: LCCN 2024038348 (print) | LCCN 2024038349 (ebook) | ISBN 9798893042443 (library binding) | ISBN 9798893043419 (ebook)
Subjects: LCSH: Rock hyrax--Juvenile literature. | Rock hyrax--Life cycles--Juvenile literature.
Classification: LCC QL737.H9 B696 2025 (print) | LCC QL737.H9 (ebook) | DDC 599.6/8--dc23/eng/20240911
LC record available at https://lccn.loc.gov/2024038348
LC ebook record available at https://lccn.loc.gov/2024038349

Editor: Elizabeth Neuenfeldt Series Designer: Veah Demmin

Printed in the United States of America, North Mankato, MN.

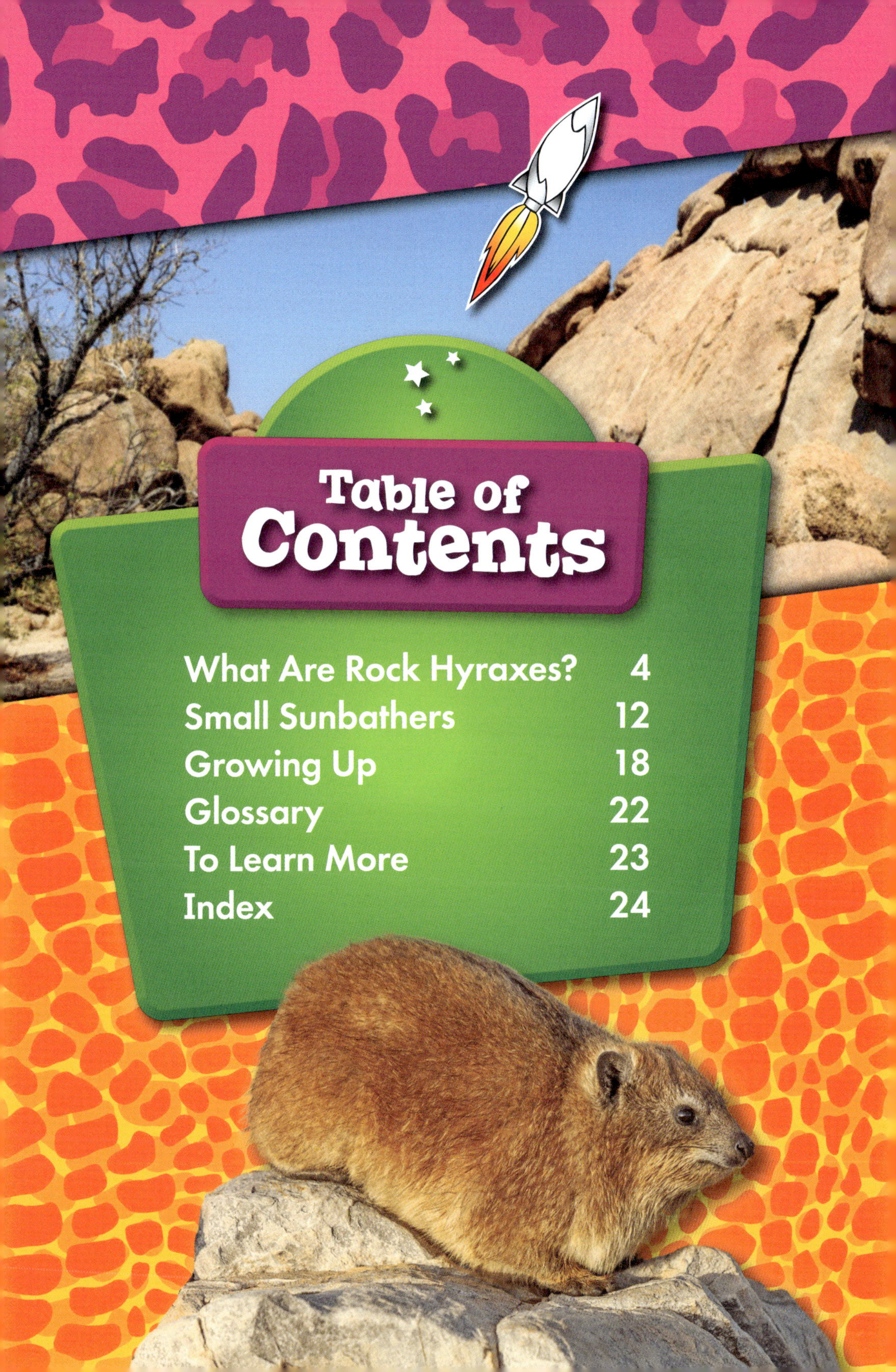

Table of Contents

What Are Rock Hyraxes?

tusks

Rock hyraxes are small **mammals**. They live in parts of Africa and western Asia. These animals have sharp **tusks**.

Rock Hyrax Report

Status in the Wild

least concern

Habitats

deserts

rocky areas

savannas

shrublands

Rock hyraxes are brown. Lighter fur covers their bellies. Their backs have patches of black fur.

They have long **guard hairs**. These help hyraxes feel things around them.

Rock hyraxes have small ears and short **snouts**.

They have special eyelids. These help **protect** hyraxes from dust.

Rock hyraxes have short legs. Their front claws are short. Longer claws on their back feet help them scratch.

The bottoms of their feet are bare. This helps them climb.

Spot a Rock Hyrax
small ears
sharp tusks
short legs

Small Sunbathers

Rock hyraxes live in **savannas** or **shrublands**. Some call rocky areas or cliffs home.

These animals live in **colonies**. A colony can have 50 hyraxes!

Rock hyraxes **sunbathe** in the morning. Then they search for food.

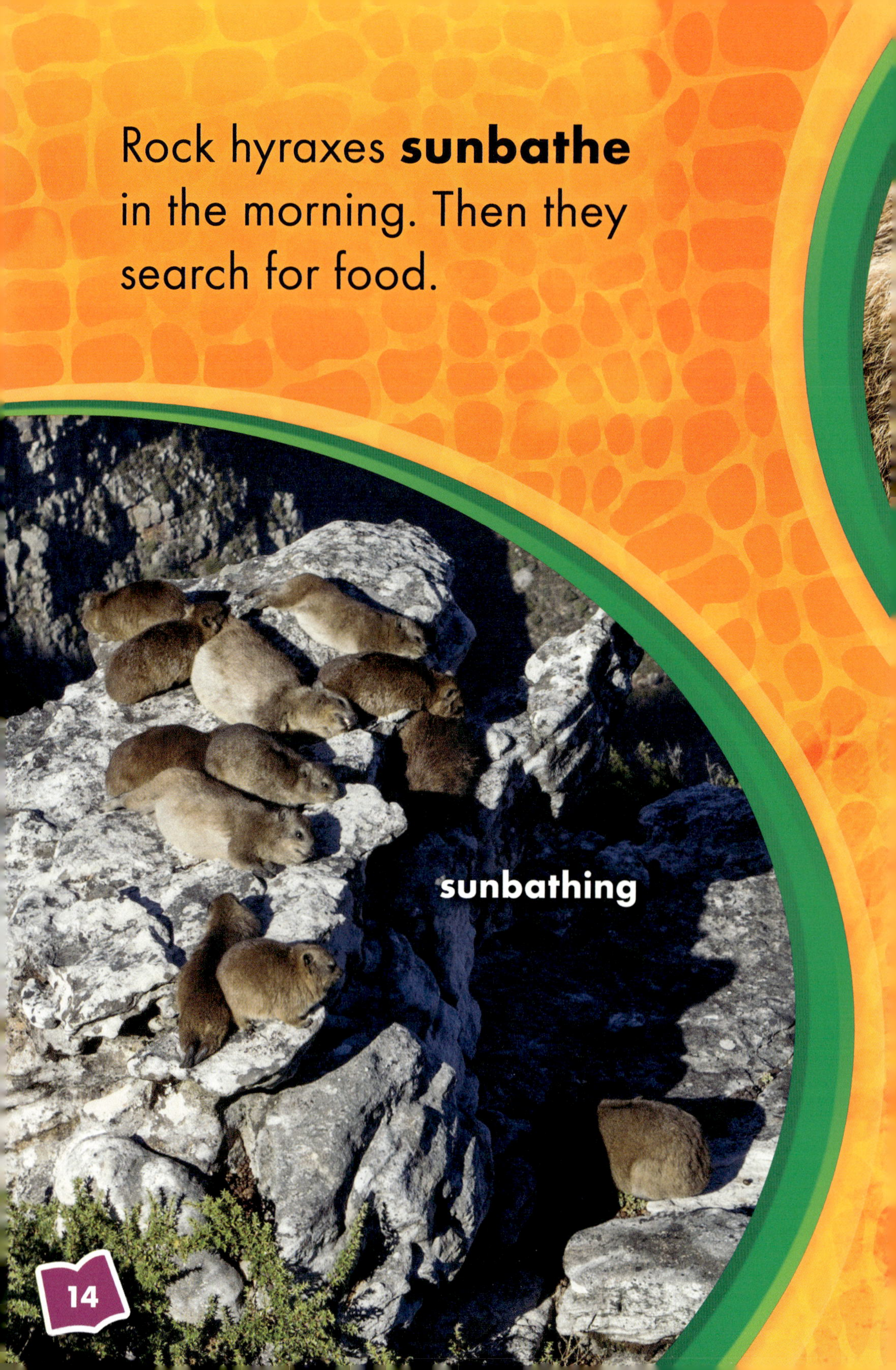

sunbathing

Hyraxes eat grass during wet seasons. They eat fruits and leaves during dry seasons.

Rock hyraxes eat together in a large circle. They watch for **predators** such as leopards and hyenas.

They also hide from snakes and eagles.

Growing Up

Female rock hyraxes give birth to **pups**. Up to six pups are born at once.

Pups stay in **nursery groups**.

pup

Rock hyrax pups can eat plants three days after birth. Soon, they learn to find their own food.

After two years,
males leave their colony.
Time to find a new one!

Life of a Rock Hyrax

Name of Babies

pups

Number of Babies

up to 6

Time Spent with the Colony

Glossary

colonies—large groups of rock hyraxes that live together

guard hairs—long, thick hairs on the outside of a rock hyrax's fur

mammals—warm-blooded animals that have backbones and feed their young milk

nursery groups—small numbers of rock hyrax pups that are cared for by the colony

predators—animals that hunt other animals for food

protect—to keep safe

pups—baby rock hyraxes

savannas—flat grasslands with few trees

shrublands—dry grasslands that have mostly low plants and few trees

snouts—the noses and mouths of some animals

sunbathe—to sit or lie in the sun

tusks—the long, curved, pointed teeth of a rock hyrax

To Learn More

AT THE LIBRARY

Joubert, Beverly. *The Ultimate Book of African Animals.* Washington, D.C.: National Geographic Kids, 2021.

Sabelko, Rebecca. *Desert Animals.* Minneapolis, Minn.: Bellwether Media, 2023.

Schell, Lily. *Marvelous Mammals.* Minneapolis, Minn.: Bellwether Media, 2023.

ON THE WEB

FACTSURFER

Factsurfer.com gives you a safe, fun way to find more information.

1. Go to www.factsurfer.com.

2. Enter "rock hyraxes" into the search box and click 🔍.

3. Select your book cover to see a list of related content.

Index

The images in this book are reproduced through the courtesy of: Thomas Noitz, front cover; AndreAnita, front cover background, interior background; Green Wall Std, front cover (rock hyrax icon); David Steele, p. 3; Shimon Bar, p. 4; Roger de la Harpe, p. 6; Cezary Wojtkowski, p. 7; Ondrej Prosicky, p. 8; Wormsmeat, p. 9; dD from Belgium, p. 10; AllyE, pp. 10-11, 13; Sanne66, p. 11; Jeff W. Jarrett, p. 11 (tusks); Buzz_v2, p. 12; MandD, p. 14; Efimova Anna, p. 15; Frederic Doucet, pp. 16-17, 17 (rock hyrax); Henk Bogaard, p. 17 (leopards); EcoPrint, pp. 17 (hyenas), 19; Stu Porter, p. 17 (snakes); Doikanoy, p. 17 (grasses); Gingertomcat, p. 17 (fruits); Md. Nadir Hasan, p. 17 (leaves); HunsaBKK, p. 18; FLPA/ Alamy, p. 20; Jens_Bee, p. 21; icons quipo, p. 21 (rock hyrax icon); Martin Pelanek, p. 23.